A Guide to
Access 2000

by

Adrian Beck

Mark Maynard

Richard Rodger

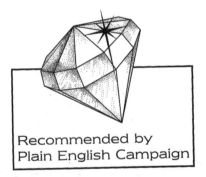

Recommended by
Plain English Campaign

Software Made Simple
3 Glenbervie Drive, Beltinge, Herne Bay, Kent CT6 6QL
Telephone: 01227 361263
Fax: 01227 371054

Internet: http://www.s-m-s.co.uk
Email: guides@s-m-s.co.uk

OTHER GUIDES IN THIS SERIES

• Excel 2000 • Word 2000 • PowerPoint 2000

• Word 97 • Excel 97 • Access 97 • PowerPoint 97

• Word 7 • Excel 7 • Access 2 • Word 6

Also Available on CD-ROM as a Site Licence

For further information please contact:

Software Made Simple
3 Glenbervie Drive, Beltinge, Herne Bay, Kent CT6 6QL

Telephone 01227 361 263
Fax 01227 371 054

Internet: http://www.s-m-s.co.uk
Email: guides@s-m-s.co.uk

This Guide assumes a basic understanding of how to use a PC and Windows. If you are not confident that you have this basic understanding then read the companion Guide: **A Guide to Word 2000** which contains the necessary information.

Version 1

Contents

1.0

INTRODUCTION

A database is a collection of information (data) which is systematically organised. There are many examples of databases in everyday life, for example, an attendance register, a shop

stock list, a telephone book. Using a database management system (database program) like Access, databases such as these can be manipulated and searched. For example, Access would allow you to sort a database of publications into alphabetical order based on the author's name, and to search for the author of a particular publication. Access can sort or find information much faster than you could by hand so looking through huge lists of information becomes a practical proposition. Data can also be manipulated using Access, eg. you could find out the total number of publications there are in the database, or how many by a particular author, or published after say, 1980.

Databases are structured into tables, records and fields. A table consists of a set of records (rows). Each record contains a number of distinct fields (columns). An example of a record would be information about a particular publication, say the book 'For Whom The Bell Tolls'. Examples of fields are the author, the publisher, and the ISBN (International Standard Book Number).

As with database programs generally, before you start to use Access you should consider carefully what information you wish to record, the form in which you wish to record it, and what data you may want to retrieve from the database.

1.1

Database Design

Database design is a big topic – entire books have been written on the subject. Traditionally it has been viewed as a difficult task requiring highly specialised skills and consuming a great deal of time and effort. Whilst this may be true for large shared databases which have to take into account a wide range of considerations and users, small or single-user databases are not necessarily always difficult to design and implement. Outlined below are a number of principles that you should keep in mind when you are designing a database.

There are two types of database: Flat File Databases and Relational Databases. Both types can be created using Access.

Flat file databases are a simple type of database which consist of a single table of data, for example, a telephone book. While simpler in design, flat file databases can be inefficient if used to store inappropriate types of data as this can lead to a lot of repetition in the database. In such cases more than one table is required and this is termed a relational database.

Consider the example of a library loan database where a person may borrow several books. If this was to be implemented as a flat file database there would need to be a record containing details about each book including a field for the name of the borrower. If the person were borrowing six books her name would be repeated six times in the database alongside the records of the six books borrowed. In addition the database would need to store the Person's library card number and the loan date. Of course each of these would also have to be stored six times – not very efficient. While with a small-scale database this may not seem important, the larger the database grows the more cumbersome it becomes to search and manipulate.

In a relational database details about the book would be kept in a separate table from those of the borrower; in this way the tables can be linked (related) together by a single common field. This linking field is the only repetition required between the tables and this is much more efficient.

The key to relational databases is the process of deciding which tables you should have in the database, how these tables are related, and what fields those tables should contain. A frequent problem in the design of databases is that too few tables are used which can lead to them becoming overloaded or difficult to search, update and expand.

You need to consider carefully the sorts of questions you will want to ask the database and the types of output you will require. Very often you may have to review the design.

1.2

Stages in Creating a Database

1   Decide upon the design of your database. Section 1.1.

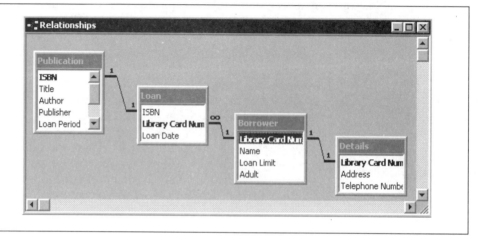

2   Create the required tables based upon your design and define the fields within each table. Section 2.3.

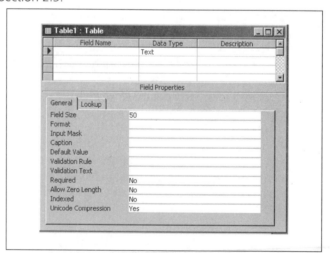

3   Enter the data for the database

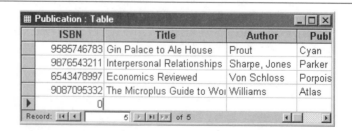

4   If you wish to make data entry easier create a Form. Section 5.0

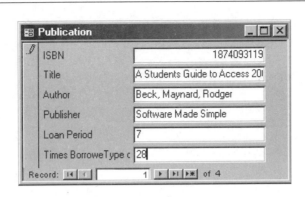

5   Search the database using a Query. Section 4.0.

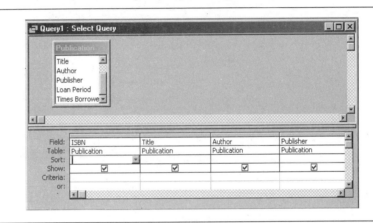

6   If you wish to print any data from the database as anything other than a simple listing use a Report. Section 6.0.

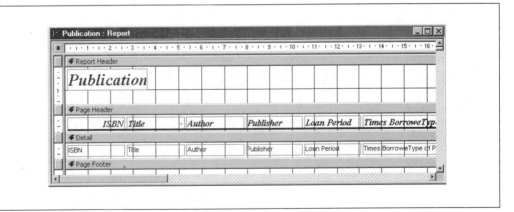

Sample Database

Throughout this guide the examples are based on a database designed to operate a local library loan system. The purpose of the database is to enable the library to store and retrieve information about which publications are on loan and to whom.

The following information needs to be recorded about the publications available: which publications are on loan, to whom, and details about people registered to use the library. Each has been logically allocated to one of four tables with the linked element underlined:

Publication:	ISBN, Title, Author, Publisher, Loan Period, Times Borrowed, Type of Publication, On Loan.
Loan:	ISBN, Library Card Number, Loan Date.
Borrower:	Library Card Number, Name, Loan Limit, Adult.
Details:	Library Card Number, Address, Telephone Number.

While this may appear intimidating, examples in this guide will refer only to the Publication table unless illustrating how to relate tables together and how these can then be manipulated.

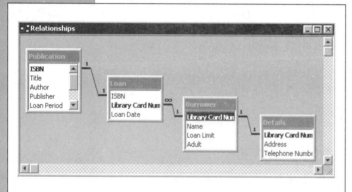

The database was divided in this way because it has broken the information which is needed into four distinct entities. The tables are linked either by the ISBN number or the Library Card Number (underlined above). Structuring the database in such a way makes it more efficient to use and reduces problems of duplication and inconsistencies.

The diagram opposite illustrates the relationship between the four tables which constitute the database.

You should note that the sample database is intended purely as an illustration and that some licence has been taken.

2.0 STARTING ACCESS

Unlike most programs where it is possible to get started with little background knowledge, the same is not true of a relational database program. Getting the initial design of the database right is essential.

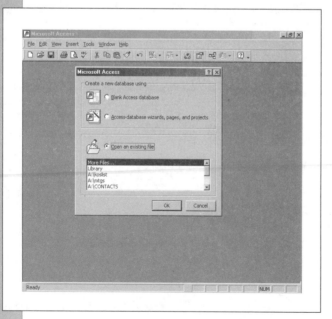

If you have not done so already, it is suggested that you read Section 1.0 of this guide and if you are still in any doubt then read a book about database design.

To begin using Access choose **Programs** from the **Start** menu and **Microsoft Access** from the sub-menu or click on the **Access button** on the **Office shortcut bar**.

The following window is displayed.

There are two ways of starting Access:

• Using a database which has already been set up (see Section 2.2).

• Setting up a new database (see Section 2.3).

2.1

The Office Assistant – Help Using Access

By default Access will probably display the **Office Assistant**. The Office Assistant is shown as an animated character and clicking once on the character will display a speech bubble into which you can type a question relating to the workings of Access. Click on the **Search** button and the Office Assistant will try and answer your question. Usually a selection of possible answers is returned, and for further details just click on the most appropriate answer.

Note: If for any reason the Office Assistant is not displayed, click on the [?] button on the Toolbar. Conversely, to **hide the Office Assistant** choose Hide the Office Assistant from the **Help** menu.

While you work the Office Assistant monitors the way you use Access. If it has suggestions that may assist you a light bulb is displayed alongside the character and clicking on the light bulb will display the suggestion.

In addition to the Office Assistant help with any object on the screen can be obtained by choosing **What's This** from the **Help** menu and clicking on the object. More detailed help is available by choosing **Contents and Index** from the **Help** menu.

2.2

Opening an Existing Database

You may have experience of inputting data or working with an Access database created by someone else. If you wish to adapt an existing database or modify one that you have already created. In either case if Access has just started up you will be presented with a dialogue box similar to the one shown below.

If the database you wish to open has been in use recently then it may be listed in the dialogue box. In this case simply choose the database and click on **OK**.

If the database you wish to open is not listed then choose **More Files** and on **OK**. From the dialogue box presented you should find the database file. To open a file on a particular disc choose the disc by clicking on the arrow alongside the **Look in** box and double-click on the disc from those listed. If the file was saved into a particular folder double-click on the folder from those listed and when the desired file name appears in the dialogue box, open it either by clicking on the file name and then on the **Open** button, or by double-clicking the file name.

If the dialogue box above is not displayed choose **Open** from the **File** menu or click on the button on the Toolbar. The dialogue box below will appear from which you can open the required database file.

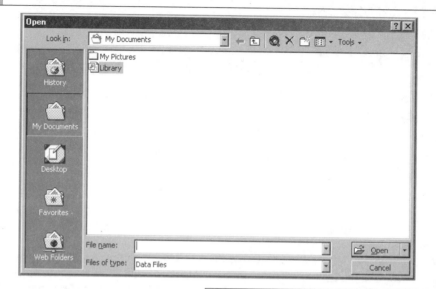

Once a database is open the Database window is displayed and from this you can choose which type of database object you wish to use. If you wish to view data in a datasheet click on the **Tables** button, choose the table you wish to view and click on the **Open** button. Similarly, if you wish to view data as a form click on the **Forms** button, choose the form you wish to view and click on the **Open** button.

Note: The distinction between a datasheet and a form is made later in the guide.

Creating a New Database

2.3

To create a new database you must decide whether to begin from scratch with a blank database or to be guided in creating the database by the **Database Wizard**. The Database Wizard provides several ready-made databases templates (see Section 2.4), if your information is consistent with one of these templates then using the Database Wizard is certainly the easiest way to create your database.

Databases created using the database wizard can be modified to suit your particular requirements both during and after creation, though this can be complicated, and ultimately more time consuming than creating a database from scratch.

If Access has just started up you will be presented with a dialogue box similar to the one shown above in Section 2.2. Click on **Blank Access Database** unless you wish to use one of the templates described below, in which case click on **Access database wizards, pages and projects.** Where Access has not just started up choose New from the File menu. In either case the dialogue box below will be displayed with either the **General** or **Databases** tab to the fore.

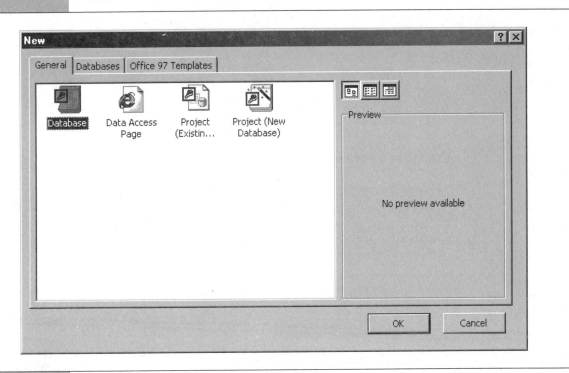

2.4 Creating a Database Using the Database Wizard

To determine whether the database you wish to create corresponds with one of the Database Wizard templates ensure that the dialogue box displayed has the **Databases** tab to the fore.

If one of the templates is suitable choose it and click on the **OK** button. In the dialogue box which follows you must decide where to save the database file and title it appropriately (for more detail see Section 7.0).

You will then be presented with a series of dialogue boxes, the responses to which allow you to customise the database to your requirements. For example, you can choose from a variety of pre-defined tables and fields whether to include sample data, and you can then choose the style used to display the data.

Note: A database created using the Database Wizard is no different to one created from scratch. If you wish to add fields; change the names of tables, or alter the appearance of the database just use the techniques outlined in the following sections.

2.5

Creating a Database from Scratch

By default your database will usually be saved to a folder called **'My Documents'** on the hard disc or network disc. If you wish to save to a different disc click on the down-arrow alongside the **Save In** box and choose the disc from those listed. If you wish to save to a different folder double-click on the folder from those listed in the dialogue box.

Next replace the default file name **'db1'** in the file name box with an appropriate file name for your database.

Click on **Create** to create the database.

The tables of the database must now be created.

2.6

Creating Tables

To create a table you must decide whether to begin with a blank table or to be guided in creating the table by the **Table Wizard**. The Table Wizard provides many ready-made tables for you to use and, as with database templates, if this suits your purpose it is certainly the easiest way to create tables. However, more likely than not your data will not conform to one of these ready made tables and you will then need to create your own table from scratch.

To create a table click on the **Tables** button in the **Database** window and choose **Create table in Design view, Create table by using wizard** or **Create table by entering data** and click on the **New** button.

2.7

Creating a Table using the Table Wizard

To determine whether the table you wish to create corresponds with one of the pre-defined tables, choose Create table by using wizard. A series of dialogue boxes is presented; the first displays the pre-defined tables and associated fields.

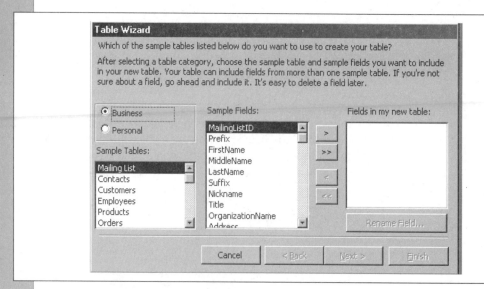

If one of the sample tables shown on the left of the dialogue box is suitable choose it and examine the associated sample fields. If all the fields in each of the tables are suitable for use in your database, click on the >> button to nominate them as fields in your table. Alternatively, for each field which is suitable, select the field and click on the > button. Repeat this for each field you wish to use in the table. If none of the tables is suitable click on **Cancel** and create your table from scratch (see Section 2.8).

Note: You can construct your table using sample fields from different sample tables.

Fields may be removed from use using the < button. All fields from a particular table may be removed by clicking on the << button.

Fields may be renamed by selecting them from the **Fields in my new table** section of the dialogue box and clicking on the **Rename Field** button. Simply enter the alternative into the dialogue box presented.

Subsequent Table Wizard dialogue boxes require you to name the table, decide upon how the primary key is specified (Section 2.13), establish any relationships between this and any other tables (Section 2.14) and finally decide how to proceed when the table is created.

2.8 Creating a Table from Scratch

To create a table from scratch choose **Design View** from the **New Table** dialogue box. A new table will be created as below. It is at this stage that the fields of the table are defined (see Section 2.9).

More than one table can be created in this way but first the current table must be titled and saved. Saving in Access is different from other programs. For information about saving see Section 7.0.

To close a table you no longer wish to use choose **Close** from the **File** menu.

2.9 Defining Fields

Database tables use a number of categories or fields in which data is stored. Library catalogues – cards with author's name, title of publication, publisher, date of publication – are a case in point of a physical database now increasingly replaced by an electronic one. Each element – name, title, publisher etc. is a field, and these must be defined before data can be entered.

To define fields a table needs to be viewed in **Design View**. If you using a view other than design view the left-most button on the Toolbar will be displayed as ☒ . Click on this button to switch to design view.

From the design view window the fields common to every record of the database are defined.

To define a field, type the name you have chosen for the field into the column beneath **Field Name**. Long field names can be accommodated by increasing the width of the column. To do this move the pointer to the line which divides the titles of the Field Name and Data Type columns. The pointer will change shape. Now click and drag right to widen the column as required.

Press the **Tab** (→/) key to move to the **Data Type** column and choose a data type by clicking on the down-arrow ▾ and making your choice from the pop-up menu. Definitions of the field data types are provided in Section 2.10. Press the **Tab** (→/) key to move on to the Description column where you may if you wish include a full description of the field.

Enter Field Name Here   Enter Data Type Here

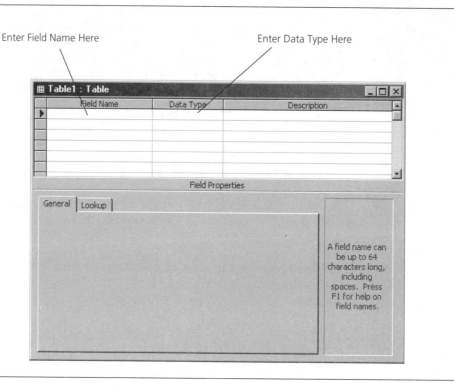

Hint: For a shortcut to entering text field data type press the **Enter** (⏎) key after typing the field name. This enters the Text data type automatically.

Move to the next field by pressing the **Tab** (→/) key or by using the mouse. Repeat this procedure for as many fields as you wish to define for the table.

Once all the fields are defined close the table. You will be prompted to save your changes and these will be saved to the database file.

Note: It is advisable to define all fields at this stage though new fields can be added at any time. Similarly, the data types and options described below can generally be re-defined at any stage. For advice on good practice in database design see Section 1.0.

2.10 Data Types

To cope with various forms of data, fields are defined with different characteristics or data types. There are ten data types; each has particular advantages and disadvantages, and associated options.

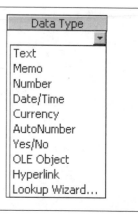

Text – Used for anything that you can type - letters, numbers or other keyboard symbols. However, without further definition numbers typed into a text field cannot be used in calculations. Limited to 255 characters. Examples of text fields in the sample database are Title and Author.

Memo – Also used for anything that you can type, such as sentences or paragraphs. Limited to 64,000 characters.

Number – Primarily used for entering numerical data. Number fields can be specified to include commas to denote thousands, a specific number of decimal places etc. An example of a number field in the sample database is the Times Borrowed field which records the number of times a publication has been borrowed.

Date/Time – The Loan Date is an example of a date/time field in the sample database.

Currency – Monetary values.

AutoNumber – A numeric value which is automatically increased for each new record.

Yes/No – Boolean values. An example of a yes/no field in the sample database is Adult, which indicates whether a borrower is an adult or not.

OLE Objects – Used to embed objects from other programs into a database.

Hyperlink – Text used as a link to a file or page of data.

Lookup Wizard – Permits you to choose a value from another table or from a list of values from a list or combo box. The Lookup Wizard creates a Lookup field and the data type set is based upon the values chosen in the wizard.

2.11

Setting the Properties of a Field

By setting the field property you can ensure that Access automatically records values entered into these fields in your preferred format. For example, dates in the 3rd June 2000 format instead of 03/06/2000 or £1,000 instead of 1000.

To alter the property of a field:

- Ensure that the table is in Design View.

- Select the field for which you wish to set the property by clicking on the Field Selector to the left of the field.

Field Selector

Properties for this field are entered here

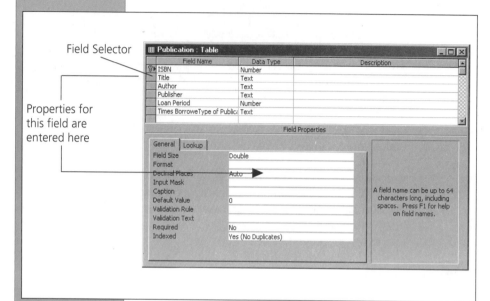

The current properties of the field are displayed in the lower pane of the window.

- Click in the box of the property you wish to change and enter a value. Typical values for most data types are listed below. Some properties display a pre-define list of values. To use these click on the down arrow ▾ which appears and make your choice from the property types displayed in the pop-up menu.

Note: Any properties defined for data in a table are automatically also applied to Queries, Forms and Reports. However, properties which relate to each of these database objects can also be set independently.

Format Properties

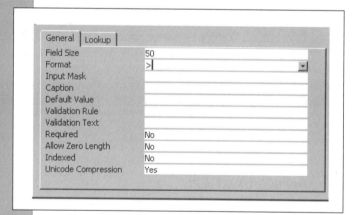

The most commonly used text property is to enter > to display entered text as upper case, enter < to display entered text as lower case.

Common property types for numbers, dates and currency are available from the pop-up menu. Alternatively for numbers/currency enter a typical property with zeros representing the numbers, eg. 0,000.00 would display 1234.5 as 1,234.50.

Entering a Default Value

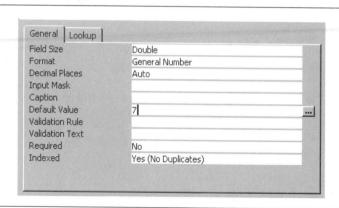

Automated data entry is valuable: it avoids typing errors and ensures accuracy. Where a particular field contains a common value in every record it is very useful to have Access add that value automatically to any new record. In this way the value need only be changed on the odd occasion that it differs from the default, so speeding up data entry.

Click on the **Default Value** property and enter the value you wish to use as a default. For example using the sample database, the Loan period field could be set to a default value of 7 representing the usual one week loan.

Enforcing or Limiting Data Entry

It can be tempting when entering data into a database to omit information which is not easily to hand. The resulting incomplete data can lead to inaccuracies when querying the database. To avoid any omissions in data the **Required** property can be used by setting this property to **Yes**.

If you wish to limit the data which may be entered into a field the **Validation Rule** property can be used. For example you may wish to limit what is entered into the Type of Publication field to Book or Article. To do this enter each of the permitted values separated by or, ie. Book or Article. Now if any other than the permitted values are entered an error will be displayed. If you wish to define the text of the error, enter this text in the **Validation Text** property. Test out the validation by changing to datasheet view and entering some sample values.

Note: Null may also be entered into the Validation Rule property if you wish to permit the field to be left blank. Also note, the Validation Rule is not case sensitive.

If you wish to ensure that a number with a specific number of digits is entered use the **Input Mask** property and enter a zero for each digit. For example, 0000000000 for the 10 digit ISBN number. Text and data fields can also use input masks for these a wizard is at hand for assistance click on the button alongside the **Input Mask** property to start the Wizard.

Adding, Deleting and Modifying Fields

To modify the design of a table ensure that it is being viewed in design view. To modify a field within the table select the field and then modify the field name, data type and description as required. To re-order a field, click on the **Field Selector** to the left of the field name and drag the field to its new position in the field order.

To adjust the width of a column so as, for example, to view a long field name, move the pointer to the line which divides the titles of the columns you wish to resize. The pointer will change shape. Click and drag right or left to resize the column as required.

To insert a new field, select the field above which you wish to create a new field and click on the ◱ button on the Toolbar. To delete a field select it and click on the ◱ button on the Toolbar.

Important: Be careful when deleting fields and re-defining a fields data type for a table already containing data. If the data cannot be fitted to the new data type it may be permanently modified eg. re-defining a text field as a number field would delete all alphabetic characters entered into the field.

Changes such as those above are permanent and there is no way to recover data.

2.13

Setting the Primary Key in a Table

Once you have defined all the fields of a table you should set its Primary Key. The Primary Key is allocated to a field which identifies uniquely each record in the table (it is often an identification number or product code). The Primary Key will determine the order of records in a table and its main advantage is that it will speed up the querying (searching) of your database.

To Set a Primary Key:

When you close a newly created table, and before saving, Access gives you the opportunity to set the Primary Key yourself or have Access do it for you. If you choose the latter Access will create a new field that will generate a unique consecutive number for each record. This may not always be appropriate as in many cases a field containing a unique identifier will already exist.

To define your own Primary Key select the field you wish to use and click on the ⚷ button on the Toolbar. A key symbol will appear alongside the field name.

To change the Primary Key to another field repeat the procedure above.

To use our sample database:

In our sample database the Primary Keys for each table were set as the ISBN number for each publication or the Library Card Number. Both of these are unique to each record in the database.

Primary Key

Field Name	Data Type	
⚷ ISBN	Number	
Title	Text	
Author	Text	
▶ Publisher	Text	
Loan Period	Text	
Times BorroweType of Publicɑ	Text	

If required you may specify more than one field as the primary key. To do this simply select these fields by holding down the **Ctrl** key while selecting.

Note: While records are placed in Primary Key order this does not take effect until the table is closed and re-opened.

2.14

Table Relationships

If you have created a number of tables which are linked you may wish to establish a relationship between the tables. Building a relationship allows information in different tables to be combined meaningfully.

Access can set up two types of relationship between tables: One-to-One and One-to-Many. A third type of relationship called a Many-to-Many relationship exists but can only be accommodated through changes in the design of the database. Many-to-Many relationships are beyond the scope of this guide.

In order to build a relationship between two tables it is necessary for the tables to have a field in common. The fields need not necessarily have the same name but they must contain the same data. The common field is usually, but not necessarily, the primary key.

The most commonly found relationships are One-to-Many. In a One-to-Many relationship a record in one table can be matched to many records in a second table. However, a record in the second table can only be related to one record in the first. Using our example, one library user may have many publications on loan in the Loan table.

In a One-to-One relationship a record in one table can be matched to no more than one record in a second table, and vice versa. Using our example one record in the Borrower table is associated with one record in the Details table.

Creating a Relationship Between Tables

- While the Database window is displayed click on the ⛓ button on the Toolbar. This displays the **Relationships** window.

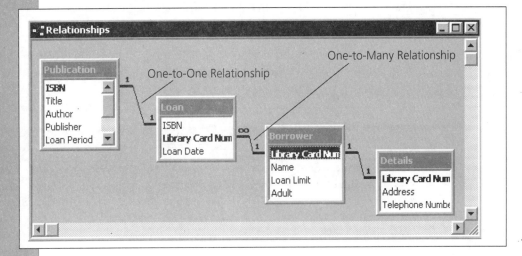

To establish relationships between tables choose **Show Table** from the **Relationships** menu. The Show Table dialogue box is displayed.

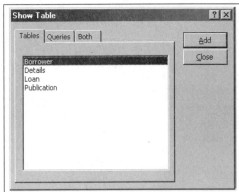

- From the dialogue box choose each table you wish to establish a relationship between and click on the **Add** button. Click on the **Close** button when you have finished. Any tables added will appear in the Relationships window.

- To create a relationship drag the field you wish to relate from one table to the matching field on the other.

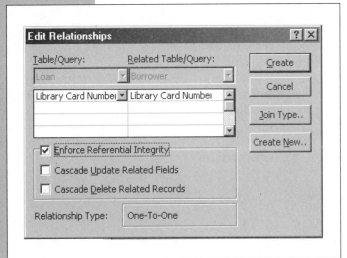

- From the dialogue box displayed click on the **Enforce Referential Integrity** box if you are joining two primary keys. In addition Access displays the relationship type between the two tables. Click on **Create** to establish the relationship.

- In the Relationships window lines (joins) are shown between the tables indicating their relationship. A 1 at the beginning and end of a join indicates a **One-to-One** relationship. A 1 at the one end of a join and a ∞ at the other indicates a **One-to-Many** relationship.

3.0

ENTERING DATA INTO A TABLE

Once fields have been defined the database is just an empty shell awaiting the entering of data.

Data is generally entered into a table while in datasheet view so ensure that **Datasheet** is highlighted in the **View** menu.

A Datasheet is displayed consisting of a grid showing the previously defined field names above each column. Information (data) relating to the fields of records is then entered one row at a time.

Data can be entered at the insertion point. To move between fields either click on the field where you wish to enter data, or press the **Tab** (→/) key to move to the next field.

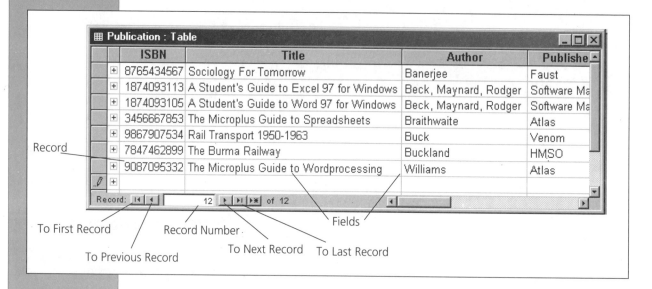

Use the same method to move on to a new record that is always displayed beneath the previous record.

Note: Unless you specify otherwise it is not necessary to enter data into every field of a record.

If there are more fields per record than can be displayed in the window the scroll-bars along the side and/or bottom of the window become active. Use these scroll-bars as you would with any other program. Similarly use the scroll-bars to view records not currently displayed in the window.

Data entered into a table is automatically saved each time the insertion point is moved on to the next record.

Creating a **Form** provides a more accessible way of entering data into a database than using a datasheet. See Section 5.0 for more about Forms.

3.1 Using Cut, Copy and Paste

Cut, Copy and Paste can be used to move or copy data around the datasheet or between tables:

- Select the data you wish to move.

- If you wish to move the data choose **Cut** from the **Edit** menu. The data will disappear.

- Alternatively, if you wish to copy the data choose **Copy** from the **Edit** menu.

- Move the insertion point to where the data is to be placed and choose **Paste** from the **Edit** Menu. The data will appear at the insertion point.

Note: You may paste your data as many times as required.

3.2 Selecting in the Datasheet

Select a single record (row) by clicking on the **Record Selector** to the left of the record.

Select multiple records by clicking on the record selector of the first record of the selection and dragging down to the last record you wish to select.

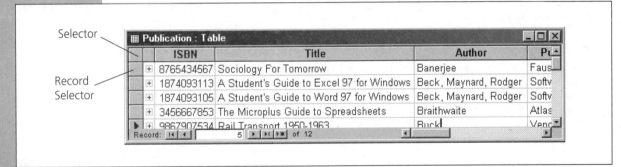

Select all records by clicking on the **Selector** in the upper left corner of the datasheet.

To select a field (column) contained within all records click on the particular field name at the top of the datasheet.

3.3 Adding, Deleting and Modifying a Record

Data entered into a field can be edited in the same way as you would with a word-processor. Use the mouse to move the insertion point within the field, and then type, delete or amend data as required.

To delete an entry in a field altogether click on the left edge of the field and press the **Delete** (Del) or **Backspace** (←) key.

To delete a complete record, select it and press the **Delete** (Del) key.

3.4

The Undo Command

One useful facility you will soon grow to love is **Undo**. This is available by clicking on the ↰ button on the Toolbar.

Undo undoes the last thing that you did. So if you made a new entry or altered an existing one and changed your mind, use the Undo command. However, remember unlike many other programs, Access can only undo the last thing that you did.

Clicking on the Undo button for a second time will redo what was undone.

4.0

MANIPULATING THE DATABASE

The intrinsic power of databases is based on the searching, sorting and cross-matching of records, often from more than one table, and performing calculations based on data stored in a number of individual records. For example, a mail order company may seek to obtain a list of individuals who subscribe to particular magazines and, before targeting potential customers, wish to list those customers who fit into a particular income bracket or professional group.

4.1

Sorting and Filtering

Each record is stored in a table in the order in which it was entered. However, this may not be the order in which you wish to browse the records. By sorting a table you can temporarily rearrange the records according to certain criteria. Alternatively, you may wish to temporarily browse only those records which conform to certain criteria. To achieve this you can filter the table.

Sorting and filtering differ from querying in that they are temporary and based only upon a single table, whereas a query can be saved and can be based upon several tables.

4.2

Performing a Quick Sort

To sort a single table based on one or more fields or to sort a form based on a single field the technique below is used. For more complex sorting see Section 4.3.

To sort a table based on a single field:

• Ensure that you are viewing the table in Datasheet or Form View by choosing the appropriate command from the **View** menu.

• Select the field you wish to sort by clicking on the name of the field at the top of the Datasheet window or by selecting the field in the form.

		ISBN	Title	Author	Publisher
▶	+	8765434567	Sociology For Tomorrow	Banerjee	Faust
	+	1874093113	A Student's Guide to Excel 97 for Windows	Beck, Maynard, Rodger	Software Made
	+	1874093105	A Student's Guide to Word 97 for Windows	Beck, Maynard, Rodger	Software Made
	+	3456667853	The Microplus Guide to Spreadsheets	Braithwaite	Atlas
	+	9867907534	Rail Transport 1950-1963	Buck	Venom
	+	7847462899	The Burma Railway	Buckland	HMSO
	+	7654345677	Encaustic Floor Surfaces	Pointer	RGR press
	+	9585746783	Gin Palace to Ale House	Prout	Cyan
	+	9876543211	Interpersonal Attraction	Sharpe, Jones	Barker

Publication : Table

Record: 1 of 12

Datasheet prepared for a sort based upon Publisher Field

4.3

- To apply an ascending sort click on the ⬆ button on the Toolbar; for a descending sort click on the ⬇ button.

A sort may be performed on several adjacent fields while in datasheet view by selecting the required fields. The left-most field is sorted first. While using a form it is only possible to sort on one field at a time.

More Complex Sorting and Filtering

Occasionally it may be necessary to perform a more complex sort on your table, perhaps sorting some fields in ascending order others in descending order. Also you may wish to filter your data in order to browse only a sub-set of the total data available. In these cases you should use the method outlined below:

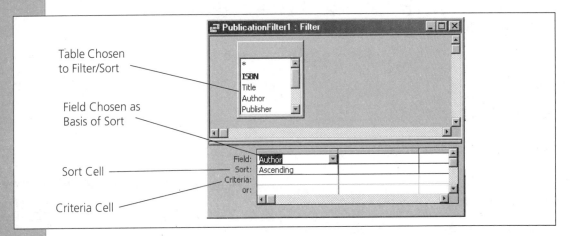

Table Chosen to Filter/Sort

Field Chosen as Basis of Sort

Sort Cell

Criteria Cell

- Choose **Filter** from the **Records** menu and **Advanced Filter/Sort** from the sub-menu. This will present the Filter window.

- Double-click on each of the field names you wish to use in your criteria for the sort/filter. These will in turn appear in the lower half of the window.

- A sort order can be applied to each field by clicking in the Sort cell below the field name, clicking on the down-arrow ▾ which appears, and choosing a sort order from the resulting pop-up menu.

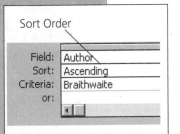

Sort Order

- Filtering criteria can be applied to each field by entering this in the Criteria cell below the field name. For example, to find all the publications by the author Braithwaite, enter Braithwaite in to the criteria cell.

  For more information on specifying criteria see Section 4.4.

- To sort or filter choose **Apply Filter/Sort** from the **Filter** menu.

  To return to the order in which each record was entered choose **Remove Filter/Sort** from the **Records** menu.

Note: Advanced Filter/Sort is also available for use with forms.

Using Queries to Find Data

One of the most powerful features of a relational database program is its query facility. A query is used to search through the database to locate a particular record or records which conform to specified criteria. These are collected into a special kind of table called a Dynaset.

This section of the guide describes how to create the Select Query as this is the most commonly used type of query. Access is capable of other types of query but these are beyond the scope of this guide.

The Select Query

Here we use the Simple Query Wizard to create a Dynaset consisting of fields from any table or tables of the database. This is displayed either as a detailed query - showing every field of every record in the Dynaset, or as a summary query - where the contents of fields may be totalled in a sum, averaged, or the minimum and maximum values of a field displayed.

Here we use a query on our database to show the books on loan to each borrower.

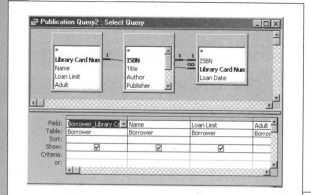

The query can be further refined by modifying it in design view. This permits you to limit the records displayed in the Dynaset depending on certain criteria and to determine how those records are displayed. For example, you could display details of those books borrowed by a particular person, or how many books the student had borrowed for more than one week. You could also choose to display records in a particular sort order.

Creating a Select Query

Here we use a wizard to assist us in creating our query

* To create a Select Query click on the **Queries** button in the database window, choose **Create query by using wizard** and click on the **New** button.

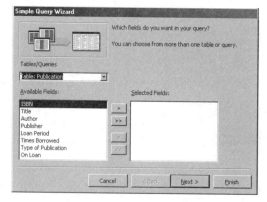

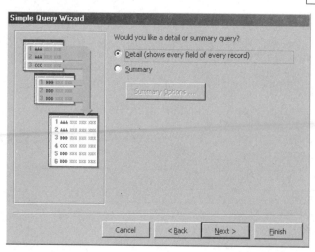

* From the resulting Simple Query Wizard dialogue box choose a table containing fields you wish to use in the query from the **Tables/Queries** pop-up menu. Next, click on each of the fields from the table that you wish to use in the query and on the ▷ button. If you wish to use all fields from the table in your query click on the ▷▷ button. To use fields from another table in your query simply choose the table from the Tables/Queries pop-up menu and repeat the procedure above. Click on the **Next** button when you have added all the required fields.

- The following dialogue box requires you to choose whether you wish to display a detailed or summary query. If you click on **Summary**, a **Summary Options** button is available and clicking on this displays the dialogue box below.

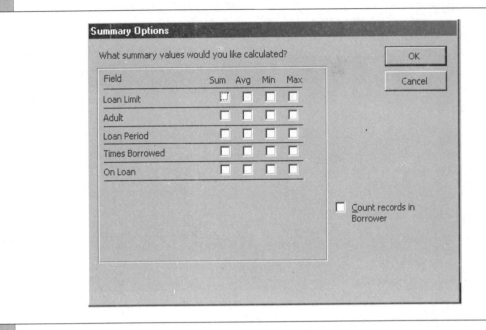

- The dialogue box allows you to choose the types of summary you require for each of the chosen fields. For example using our sample database you might wish to have a query find the average number of times books are borrowed.

- Clicking on the **Next** button displays the last dialogue box of the Simple Query Wizard.

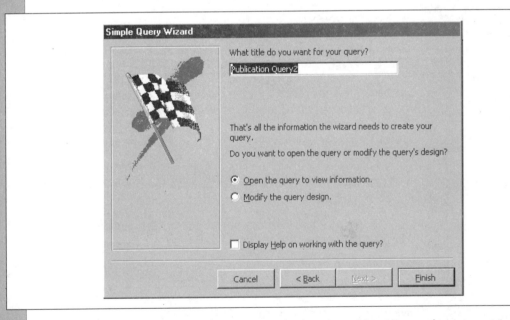

Enter a name for your query and choose whether you wish to **Open the query to view information** or **Modify the query design**. If you wish to refine the query in the manner described above then click on the latter button. If you choose to view the information but later decide to you wish to refine the query simply click on the button on the Toolbar.

- Lastly, click on the **Finish** button and the result of the query will be opened as a datasheet or in query design view depending upon the options chosen.

4.4

Refining the Query

Refining a query permits you to sort the contents of fields and add criteria to your select query. For example, using our sample database you might wish to view the titles of all books borrowed more than 100 times or perhaps view the types of publication borrowed by a particular person.

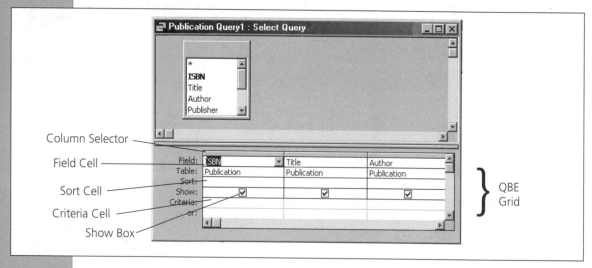

Column Selector
Field Cell
Sort Cell
Criteria Cell
Show Box

QBE Grid

To refine a query follow the procedure below.

*   Open the query in design view to display the Select Query window.

*   Tables used in the query are displayed in the top half of the window. Where more than one table is used they will be joined together with lines which reflect the relationship which was established when the tables were created, see Section 2.14. However, if desired, the relationship between tables can be changed in the Select Query window.

*   Fields and any criteria for the query are added to the Query By Example (QBE) grid which occupies the lower half of the Select Query window. Field names are prefixed by the name of the table to which the field belongs.

*   A sort order can be applied to each field by clicking first in the Sort cell below the field name, then by clicking on the down-arrow ▾ which appears, and finally by choosing a sort order from the resulting pop-up menu. The leftmost field on the QBE grid is sorted first. To alter the sort order select the column containing the field you wish to move by clicking on its Column Selector and dragging the column to its new position in the order.

*   If you wish a field to be included in the query but not displayed in the Dynaset (eg. to be used as part of a calculation, see Specifying Criteria in a Query below) click in the Show box under the field you do not wish to display.

*   Clicking on the Datasheet button on the Toolbar causes all data from the fields specified on the QBE grid to be displayed in a Dynaset.

*   If you wish to return to the Select Query window, perhaps to refine your query further, click on the button on the Toolbar.

Note: Any changes you make in the Select Query window are automatically reflected when you switch to the Dynaset.

*   You may wish to save your query so that it can be used again, perhaps when more data has been added to the database or when data has been modified. For information about saving refer to Section 7.0.

Specifying Criteria in a Query

- Query criteria can be applied to each field by entering this in the Criteria cell beneath the field name.

- If your criteria are simple then they can be entered directly into the criteria cell. Examples of such criteria are shown in the boxed section below.

Examples of Simple Criteria

Text Criteria

Entering text would find an exact match for the text, eg. entering Buck under the Author field would find the Author Buck but not Buckland. Unless otherwise specified text searches are not case sensitive, eg. buck and Buck are both found.

> **Note**: On leaving the criteria cell any text entered will automatically be enclosed in quotation marks.

Simple Mathematics

Access enables you to make specific query's of an arithmetic kind. How often, more than, less than and the number of occurrences between, a range of numbers can be specified easily.

If you wished to find publications which are available on loan for longer than the standard 7 days the criteria >7 can be entered under the Loan Period field.

If you wished to find publications which had been borrowed less than ten times the criteria <10 can be entered under the Times Borrowed field.

If you wished to find publications which had never been borrowed the criteria 0 can be entered under the Times Borrowed field.

- Access provides a convenient method of specifying more complex criteria by using the Expression Builder. To use the **Expression Builder** click in the criteria cell beneath the column representing the field and click on the ⚟ button on the Toolbar. This will display the Expression Builder dialogue box.

- The expression or criteria is built in the upper half of the Expression Builder dialogue box from components specified in the lower half of the dialogue box. The pane to the left lists categories of items which may be used in the expression such as tables and within tables fields, forms, reports and other queries. These are all items which are saved to the database file and are here presented as a folder structure. Double-clicking on a folder reveals the items contained within it, and these are shown in the central pane of the dialogue box.

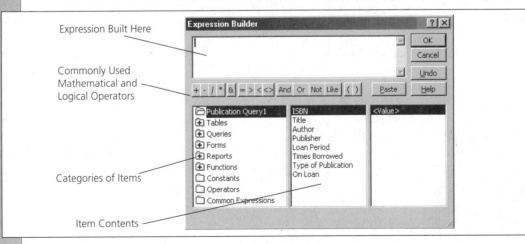

Folders displayed as ⊞ contain sub-folders. For example, double-clicking on the tables folder reveals a list of all the tables saved to the database file. Double-clicking on one of these tables reveals, in the central pane, a list of fields contained within the table.

Double-clicking on an item in the central or right pane adds it to the expression.
Items, such as those described above, can be used in conjunction with other items listed in the following folders:

Operators	eg. +, -, / (divide), * (multiply), < (less than), > (greater than), <> (equal to), And, Or, Not, Like
Constants	eg. False, True
Functions	eg. Cos, StDev, Date, In
Common Expressions	eg. Current Date

Most common mathematical and logical operators are listed on the central line of buttons in the dialogue box.

Clicking on the **OK** button inserts the expression into the Criteria cell of the Select Query window.

- If you wish to use a field in your query but not have it display as part of the Dynaset click on the **Show** box under the field name to de-select this option.

All the above examples use only a single search criterion. Below are examples of where you might want to use more than one criteria.

Note: Any text criteria are enclosed in quotes on leaving the criteria cell.

Using AND Criteria

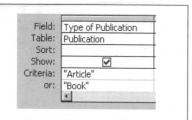

AND criteria are useful if you wish to find records based on one criterion AND another, for example, to find all publications which are articles AND which have been borrowed more than five times.

To use AND in your criteria add the required fields to the QBE grid and any criteria.

Using OR Criteria

OR criteria are useful if you wish to find records based on one criterion OR another, for example, to find all publications which are articles OR books.

To use OR in your criteria add the required fields to the QBE grid and any criteria.

Using NOT Criteria

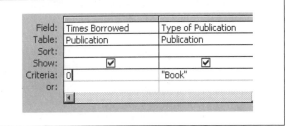

NOT is useful if you wish to find all records but NOT those which conform to a criteria, for example, to find all publications which are books but have NOT been borrowed.

To use NOT in your criteria add the required fields to the QBE grid and any criteria.

Using BETWEEN Criteria

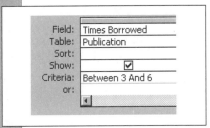

BETWEEN is useful if you wish to find all records where the data in a field is BETWEEN one value and another, for example, to find all records where the times a publication has been borrowed is between 3 and 6.

To include BETWEEN in your criteria enter BETWEEN and the range of acceptable values separated with And.

Using IN Criteria

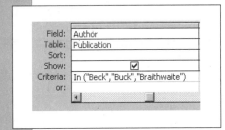

IN is useful if you wish to find all records where the data in a field is one of a set of values specified IN the criteria, for example, to find all records where the author is in the list Beck, Buck or Braithwaite.

To include IN in your criteria enter IN followed by the comma separated list of values you wish to search for enclosed within brackets.

There is almost no limit to the number of functions and operators which can be used in an expression. For a complete list of functions use the Office Assistant (Section 2.1) and enter Functions Reference.

Creating Calculated Fields

It can be useful to add a field to a query which is based upon calculations using data from other fields. For example, you might want to create a field which multiplies the Loan Period by the Times Borrowed to create a field named Number of Days on Loan.

To create a calculated field:

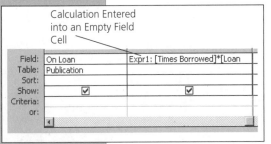

Calculation Entered into an Empty Field Cell

- Return to the Select Query window and enter the calculation into an empty field cell using the Expression Builder. You should ensure that the calculation commences with an equals symbol (=), any field names used in the expression are automatically surrounded by square brackets.

- Clicking on the **OK** button will cause Access to add its own field name to the start of the expression, eg. Expr1. This can be changed to a more meaningful name if required.

- Criteria etc. can be added to the calculated field like any other.

Using Wild Cards In Finding Text

Little flexibility is possible in the text searches described above. Exact text must be entered in the criteria cell. To find records containing text criteria no matter where in the field it might be, the **Wild Card** characters * and ? are used in combination with example text. The * symbol can be used to represent any number of characters in the text in a field, whereas the ? symbol is used to represent a single character.

For example, to search the Publication table for all publications whose author has a name beginning with the letter b, enter b* in the criteria cell. As the * symbol represents any number of characters this would find both Beck and Braithwaite.

To use ?, the single character wild card, substitute ? for any character in the text search criteria. For example, entering b?ck would find both Beck and Buck.

> **Note**: On leaving the criteria cell where a wild card has been specified then the criteria will be surrounded by quotes and prefixed by Like.

Specifying Totals in a Query

It can be useful to discover a total for a particular number field. For example, using the sample database you might wish to find out how many times several books have been borrowed. To do this from the Select Query window choose **Totals** from the **View** menu. A row of Total cells is added to the QBE grid and initially all the cells are filled with Group by. To find the total in a field click in the total cell of the field and on the down-arrow, and from the pop-up menu choose Sum or one of the other functions available.

Modifying a Query

To edit a query first ensure that the query is in Design View.

A simple query can be edited directly in the criteria cell. However you may find it more convenient to click in the criteria cell and edit more complex queries from the Expression Builder dialogue box. Click on the criteria and then on the ⟨⟩ button on the Toolbar to open the Expression Builder. Edit the expression as normal text. See Section 4.4 for more about the Expression Builder.

5.0 USING FORMS

The use of Forms provides an alternative and more accessible way of presenting and entering your data than using a datasheet. The form permits the viewing of a single record at a time, and the design of the form can be easily customised to suit your requirements.

Shown right is a typical form drawn from the publication table.

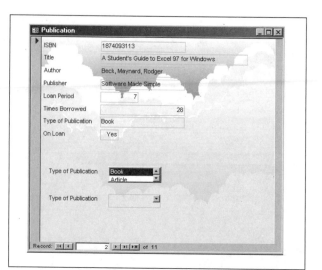

The main advantages of using a form are:

- It is familiar, as it is similar to a paper form.

- It is often quicker to enter data using a form.

- Data can be presented in a more attractive and accessible manner and can include graphs and pictures.

- Forms can display data from a table or from a query.

- Forms can be designed to display only selected data.

- Forms can be sorted or queried just like tables.

Forms can take their data from tables, queries or can be created especially for the form. Wherever the source, the data is held in the form as objects called **Controls**.

Most controls are bound to fields from the original table or query and allow data to be changed using the form as an alternative to the datasheet eg. the ISBN and Author fields in the Publication table. However, some controls are just information for display purposes, eg. labels or graphics used to enhance the appearance of the form.

Creating a Form Automatically

The quickest way to create a form is to use the **Form Wizard**.

If you wish to create a form from more than one table then the answer is to create a query from which the form can be created.

- From the Database window choose the **Forms** button, click on **Create form by using wizard** and click on the **New** button.

- From the following dialogue box choose the fields upon which you wish to base the form and click on **Next**.

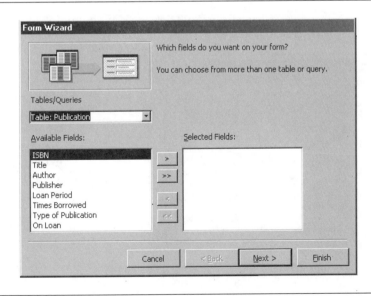

- In the next dialogue box choose the **Columnar** as the layout for your form. Click on **Next**.

> **Note**: Columnar forms are the most commonly used; other form layouts are available but these are outside the scope of this guide.

- The next dialogue box requests you to choose a style for your form from those listed. Click on **Next** when this is chosen.

- In the last dialogue box enter a name for your form and choose whether you wish to **Open the form to view information** or **Modify the form's design**. If you choose to view the information but later decide to you wish to refine the form simply click on the ![icon] button on the Toolbar.

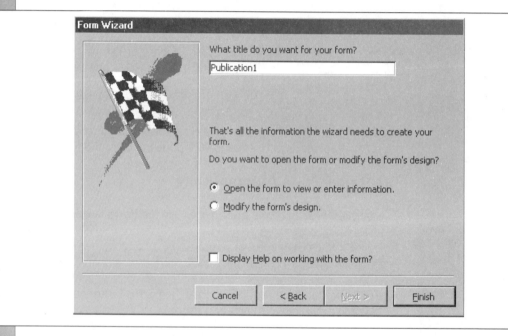

- Lastly, click on the **Finish** button and the resulting form will opened as a columnar form or in form design view depending upon the options chosen.

Shown below is a typical columnar form displaying a single record on the form. The figure illustrates how to navigate using the form.

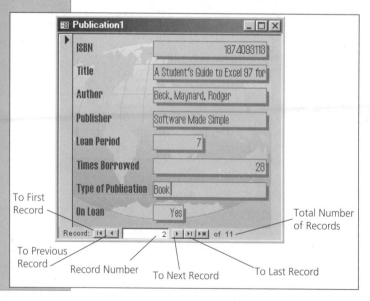

An alternative method to the above is to choose the table or query you wish your form to be based upon from the database window and click on the **New Object:AutoForm** ![icon] button on the Toolbar. However, while this method is a handy short-cut it does provide you with less control than that described above.

5.2

Refining the Form

To refine a form follow the procedure below.

- Open the form in design view. The form displayed will be similar to that shown below with the Toolbox alongside.

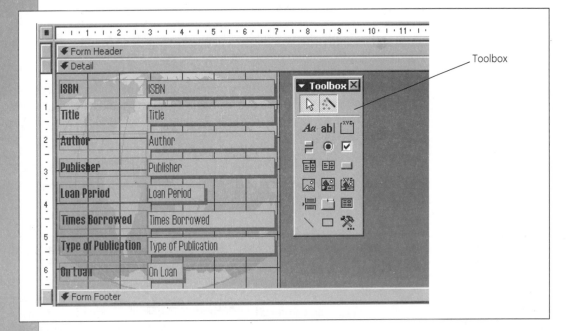

Toolbox

- Many of the operations to refine the form require the use of the Toolbox. So it is important to ensure that it is on screen. If it is not, then choose **Toolbox** from the **View** menu.

- Objects displayed on the form, like fields, are termed controls. Many are accompanied by a text label such as the field name describing the control.

Editing Controls

To resize a control or label select the object and click and drag one of the small handles (rectangles) which appear in the corners and along the sides of the object. Dragging a corner handle diagonally will resize an object in two dimensions.

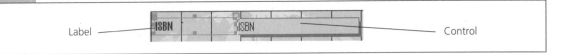

Label   Control

Note: The larger handle which appears in the top left corner of the object cannot be used for resizing.

To move a control and its label together click in the centre of either and drag them to their new position. To move the control independently of its label click on the handle in its top left corner and drag the control to its new position. You can move a label independently using the same method.

Note: Several controls can be selected at one time by clicking on the first and holding down the **Shift** (↑) key while clicking on any others. The text used in the label can be edited by clicking on the label and editing the label text as normal.

Delete a control by selecting it and pressing the **Delete** (Del) key. Labels associated with a control are deleted when the control is deleted. However the reverse is not true.

Note: Deleting a control does not delete data upon which the control is based.

Adding a Field to a Form

If you wish to add fields you decided originally to exclude from the form or that you deleted accidentally, follow the method below.

- Choose **Field List** from the **View** menu, and from the dialogue box presented choose the field or fields you wish to add to the form. To select multiple fields click on each field while holding down the **Control** (Ctrl) key. To select all fields double-click on the title of the Field List dialogue box.

- Click and drag the chosen fields from the Field List dialogue box to the form. The fields are now termed **Text Controls** and to the left of each is displayed a label showing the field name from which the control originated.

Note: Only those fields available in the table or query which are the basis of the form can be added.

Take care not to drag the field too close to the left-hand edge of the form as this will cause the text control to overwrite its label. If this happens, and it is too late to choose Undo, the text control will have to be moved independently of the label. See above.

Changing the Font, Size and Alignment of Text

Change the font, font size or alignment of text in a control by selecting it and making your choice from the Toolbar.

Positioning Objects Precisely

Access provides several tools which assist in positioning controls and other objects precisely.

By default an invisible grid is imposed on the form and controls are aligned (snapped) to this grid. Using the grid makes the positioning of objects more precise. However, occasionally you may wish to turn off the grid. To turn the grid off or on, choose the **Snap to Grid** command from the **Format** menu. With the grid turned on a appears alongside the command on the menu.

To align controls:

- Select the controls you wish to align.

- Choose **Align** from the **Format** menu and type of alignment you require from the sub-menu.

Adjusting the spacing between controls:

- Select the controls you wish to space evenly.

- Choose **Horizontal** or **Vertical** Spacing from the **Format** menu and the type of spacing you require from the sub-menu.

Creating Calculated Controls

On occasions it is useful to create a control which displays the result of a calculation involving one or more fields from a table or query.

To create a calculated control:

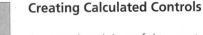

*   From the Toolbox, click on the **Text Box** tool

*   Click on the form where you wish the calculated control to appear and it will be displayed accompanied by a label.

*   Select the control and enter the calculation.

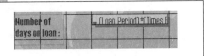

For example, as an alternative to creating the calculated field Number of Days on Loan, as above in Section 4.4, a calculated control could be used. However, a calculated control cannot be used in a query.

This would cause the calculated control to display the number of days to date a publication has been on loan. ·

Note: All field names used in calculations are surrounded with square brackets ([ ]).

For a list of functions use the Office Assistant (Section 2.1) and enter **Functions Reference**.

*   The label can be renamed so as to reflect the contents of the calculated control.

*   Calculated controls can be moved, resized and deleted as above.

Creating Label Controls

Occasionally it can be useful to create a label on its own rather than associated with any other type of control, for example, as a title. This adds a certain degree of polish to your overall presentation.

To create a label control:

*   From the Toolbox, click on the **Label** tool  .

*   Click on the form where you wish the label control to be displayed.

*   Enter the text for the label at the flashing insertion point.

To have text wrap on to a second line hold down the **Control** (Ctrl) key while pressing the **Enter** (↵) key.

*   Label controls can be moved, resized and deleted as above.

To attach a label to a control create the label as above and select the label. Choose **Cut** from the **Edit** menu, select the control to which you wish to attach the label, and choose **Paste** from the **Edit** menu.

5.3

Making Data Entry Even Easier

Entering data into a database can be an arduous and error prone task so whatever can be done to simplify this task and to improve accuracy should be employed. Using a form for data entry is a good starting point but there are refinements to the form which can also help.

Changing the Tab Order

A quick way to move between fields in a record displayed as a form is to press the **Tab** (→/) key. By default the order that the tab key uses to move between fields is the order in which they were created. To alter this order choose **Tab Order** from the View menu and in the dialogue box displayed click and drag the fields in to the required order. Click on **OK** to set the new tab order.

Setting Required and Default Values

The property type of a field can be altered to force data to be entered into a particularly important field or perhaps limit entry in some way. Also a default value can be automatically added to a field for fast entry of a commonly used value. For more information see Section 2.11.

Providing Access to Choices

It is usually easier to choose from a predefined range of options than to type your choice, and it is certainly less error prone. Access provides several ways for you to make a choice of options easier.

If you have already created a control but wish it to be displayed in one of the ways below the easiest way to achieve this is to delete the control and recreate it using the method shown.

The List and Combo Box

These provide two types of lists of choices. The **List box** provides a scrollable list of items from which to choose. The Combo box provides a pop-up menu listing items from which to choose.

The list box displays a list of choices which are displayed at all times. The list of choices in a combo box is displayed only when it is opened. Entering the first few letters of the choice into the combo box will cause it to display the closest match in the list. Also, choices not on the list can be entered.

- Click on the Control Wizard ☜ button in the Toolbox so that it is highlighted.

- Click on the List Box ▤ or Combo Box ▤ button on the Toolbox as required.

- Move the pointer to the location on the form where you wish the control to be created and click on the mouse button. The Wizard dialogue box is displayed.

Note: If no Wizard dialogue box is displayed delete the controls you have just created and start again. This time ensure that the **Control Wizard** button in the Toolbox is highlighted.

- Choose **I will type in the values that I want** and click on **Next**.

- Enter 1 as the number of columns, type the values you wish to use in your list pressing **Enter** (⏎) between each, and click on **Next**.

- Click on **Store that value in this field**, choose a field in which you wish to store the data, and click on **Next**.

- Provide a meaningful title for the controls label and click on **Finish**. The List or Combo box will be created on the form.

There are many other complex possibilities of List and Combo boxes but these are beyond the scope of this guide.

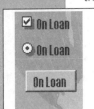

Check Boxes, Option Buttons and Toggle Buttons

These provide ways of indicating a Yes/No choice if the values for the field are defined as a Yes/No data type. This could apply in for example, the On Loan field to indicate whether a book had been borrowed by a simple Yes or No.

- Choose the type of control you wish to use, **Check box** ☑ , **Option button** ◉ or **Toggle button** ⇌ by highlighting it in the **Toolbox**.

- Choose the field you wish to use as the control from the Field List dialogue box and as normal click and drag this to the form to create the control.

- Toggle buttons can be resized in the usual way. Text can be added to a Toggle button by moving the pointer on to the button, clicking and typing.

Option Groups

These provide a way of presenting more than two choices as Check boxes, Option buttons or Toggle buttons.

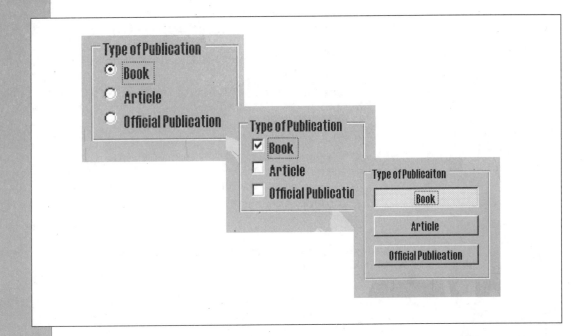

The easiest way of creating an option group is by using the Control Wizard.

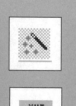

- Click on the **Control Wizard** button in the **Toolbox** so that it is highlighted.

- Click on the **Option Group** button in the **Toolbox**.

- Move the pointer to the location on the form where you wish the control to be created and click on the mouse button. The Wizard dialogue box is displayed.

- Enter the names of the items you wish to be listed as choices, and then move between each name by using the **Tab** (→/) key. When this is done click on the **Next** button.

- Choose whether you want one of the choices to be displayed as the default and click on **Next**.

- Choose which numeric value you wish associated with each choice and click on **Next**.

- Click on **Store the value in this field**, and choose a field to store the data. In the case of our example the Type of Publication field would be chosen. Click on **Next**.

- Choose which style you wish the option button to use and click on **Next**.

- Provide a meaningful title for the option group and click on **Finish**. The Option group will be created on the form.

Command buttons

These provide a way of allocating a command to a button.

Command buttons are used to initiate an action of some kind, perhaps to move on to the next record or to print a particular record. Access provides a selection of pre-defined command buttons for you to use in your form.

The easiest way of to create a Command button is by using the control wizard.

- Cick on the **Control Wizard** button in the **Toolbox** so that it is highlighted.

- Click on the **Command** button in the **Toolbox**.

- Move the pointer to the location on the form where you wish the control to be created and click on the mouse button. The Command Wizard dialogue box is displayed.

- Choose the **Category** and then the action you require when the button is pressed and click on **Next**.

- Choose how you wish the button to be displayed, with text or a pre-defined graphic and click on **Next**.

- Provide the button with a meaningful name and click on the **Finish** button. The command button will be created on the form.

Although it is possible to create buttons which undertake customised actions this is beyond the scope of this guide.

Adding Graphics

The Toolbox provides a line and rectangle tool to help you divide controls on a form into groups.

To draw a line

Click on the Line Tool ◥ , move the pointer to the position on the form where you wish to start drawing the line, and click and drag to the end of the line. When you release the mouse button the line will be drawn.

To draw a rectangle

Click on the Rectangle Tool ▭ , move the pointer to the position on the form where you wish to place one of the corners of the rectangle, and click and drag diagonally until the rectangle is the desired size. When you release the mouse button the rectangle will be drawn.

Hint: Holding down the **Shift** (⇧) key while drawing a rectangle draws a square. Holding down the **Shift** (⇧) key while drawing a line constrains the line to drawing at 90° angles.

6.0 Reporting

Reporting is how you choose to present your database as printed pages. Reports enable you to choose which fields will be printed out and which data should be included. Reports can also summarise data data in various ways. Access gives you the opportunity to design the layout of a particular report including the position of headings, field names, the data itself along with graphics such as pictures and logos. An example of a report which could be generated from our sample database would list the publications which have been borrowed and how often, perhaps providing a summary giving the total number of publications and the average number of times borrowed.

Reports can take their data from tables, queries or can be created especially for the report.

6.1 Creating a Report Automatically

The quickest way to create a report is to use the **Report Wizard**.

If you wish to create a report from more than one table then the answer is to create a query from which the report can be created.

- From the Database window choose the **Reports** button, click on **Create report by using wizard** and click on the **New** button.

- From the following dialogue box choose the fields upon which you wish to base the report. When this is complete click on the **Next** button.

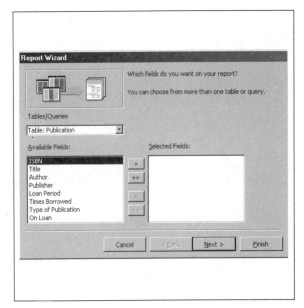

- In the next dialogue box choose any grouping levels that you wish to use, a group or level for your report. For example, you might wish to group the report into publications grouped by publisher. Click on **Next**.

- The next dialogue box requests that you choose the sort order and summary information you wish to include in your report. Use the down-arrows alongside the field boxes to choose the fields you wish to order. For example, here you might wish to sort alphabetically by author. Click on **Next**.

- In the next dialogue box chose the type of layout and orientation you would prefer for your report. Click on **Next**.

- In the next dialogue box decide upon the style of your report and click on **Next**.

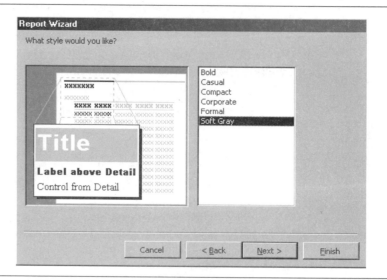

- In the last dialogue box enter a name for your report and choose whether you wish to **Preview the report** or **Modify the report's design**. If you choose to preview the information but later decide to you wish to refine the report simply click on the button on the **Toolbar**.

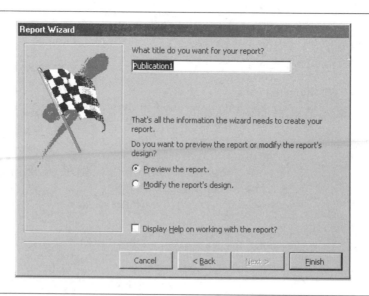

- Lastly, click on the **Finish** button and the resulting report will previewed or in report design view depending upon the options chosen.

Shown below is a section of a typical report.

Publication Details

Author	Banerjee
Title	Sociology For Tomorrow
Times Borrowed	24
Author	Beck, Maynard, Rodger
Title	A Student's Guide to Excel 97
Times Borrowed	28
Author	Beck, Maynard, Rodger
Title	A Student's Guide to Word 97

An alternative method to the above is to choose the table or query you wish your report to be based upon and click on the down-arrow alongside the **New Object**: button on the Toolbar and choose **AutoReport** from the pop-up menu. However, while this method is a handy short-cut it does provide you with less control than that described above.

• The report can be refined by using the techniques in Section 6.2.

Refining the Report

6.2

A basic report is divided into three sections – Page Header, Detail and Page Footer. Page header and footer contain data that will appear at the top or bottom of each page of the report. For example, you might wish to use this to include data about the source of the report, the date it was completed or the page number. The Detail section of the report is the most important of the sections since any controls added here display this data for every record of the database.

The sections may be adjusted in size by clicking and dragging the top edge of their title.

• Open the report in design view. The report displayed will be similar to that shown below with the Toolbox alongside.

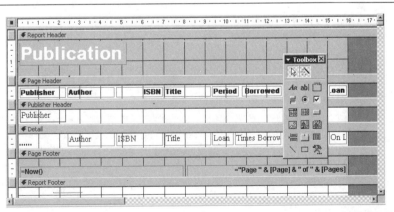

Creating, Editing and Refining Controls

The creation, editing and refining of controls in a report is exactly the same as for a form. Please refer to the relevant paragraphs in Section 5.2.

Adding Page Breaks

When printing, Access will automatically insert a new page break when no more data can be fitted on to a page. This may not always be convenient as it could result in the data contained within a record being split over two pages. To avoid this a page break can be added.

To add a page break click on 🖶 from the Toolbox and click on the report where you wish the page break to appear. The **Page Break Control** ..... symbol will appear on the report and it can be clicked and dragged into position as with any other control.

Page breaks can be deleted by selecting and pressing the **Delete** (Del) key.

Making Use of the Sections of a Report

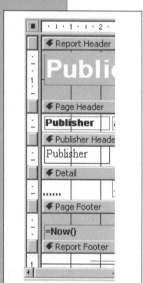

By default Access provides a report with only three sections: Header, Footer and Detail. It may be useful to add other sections, for example, a section containing a heading for the report or a section summarising figures used in the report.

There are seven types of section, and unless otherwise stated, only one of each type of section can be used in a report:

Report Header: Appears as the first page of a report. Perhaps it might be used as a preliminary page for the report.

Page Header: Appears at the top of every page of a report. Perhaps it might be used to display the title of the report.

Group Header (shown here as Publisher Header): Appears at the start of a new group of records. Perhaps this might be used to contain a description of the group. For more information about groups see below. More than one of this type of section can be added to a report. Note that the Group Header takes on the name of the particular group; here it is grouped by Publisher.

Detail Section: The main body of data.

Group Footer: Appears at the end of a group of records. Perhaps it might be used to display totals for the group of records. For more information about groups see below. More than one of this type of section can be added to a report.

Page Footer: Appears at the bottom of every page of a report, and is often used to display the page number.

Report Footer: Appears as the last page of a report, and is often used to display totals for the report, or to attach sources of data, or a bibliography.

Sections can be added or deleted by choosing **Page Header/Footer** or **Report Header/Footer** from the View menu as appropriate. However, if you delete any header or footer any controls that have been added to the section will also be deleted.

Below are typical examples which illustrate some of the most common uses of sections.

Adding a Heading to Each Page of a Report

To add a heading to the top of each page of a report the label tool is used:

- First ensure that the Page Header is displayed by checking that a ✔ appears alongside the command in the View menu. If this is not present choose the **Page Header/Footer**. This will display both a page header section and page footer section.

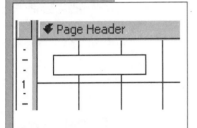

  - From the **Toolbox**, click on the **Label** tool ▣.

  - Click on the page header where you wish the label control to be displayed.

  - Enter the text for the heading at the flashing insertion point.

  - To have text wrap on to a second line hold down the **Control** (Ctrl) key while pressing the **Enter** (↵) key.

- Label controls can be moved, resized and deleted as normal.

Note: Text can be added to a Page Footer in the same way.

Adding a Page Number to Each Page of a Report

To add a page number which can be continuously and automatically adjusted, choose **Page Numbers** from the **Insert** menu.

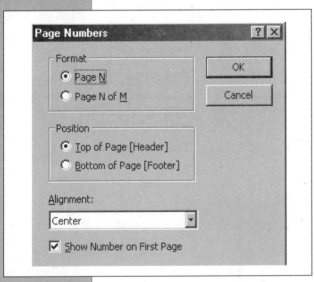

- From the following dialogue box choose the page number format, position and alignment that you require, and click on **OK**.

- The text = "Page" & [Page] or similar will appear in your report where you specified. In this case the word "Page" precedes the page number on each page.

- The page number can be moved, resized and deleted as any control.

- To check that the page number displays as required choose **Print Preview** from the **View** menu. Scroll to where you inserted the page number and it should be displayed as defined. Return to design view to further refine your report.

Note: A date and time can be added to your report in a similar manner. In this case by choosing **Date and Time** from the **Insert** menu.

Adding a Title Page to a Report

To add a title page:

- First ensure that the Report Header is displayed by checking that a ✔ appears alongside the command in the **View** menu. If it is not displayed choose the command, which will display both a report header section and report footer section.

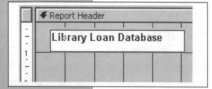

- Add your title to the report header section. It will appear only on the first page of the report.

Adding Summary Totals and Calculations to a Report

You may wish to add a page at the end of your report which provides a summary. Usually this will involve totalling particular numeric fields for all records in the report. Such data is included in a report footer. Whatever is added to the report footer section will appear only on the last page of the report when previewed or printed.

- Ensure that the Report Footer is displayed, see above.

- Add a total to the section by clicking on the **Text Box** tool ab| from the **Toolbox**.

- Click on the report footer section where you wish the calculated control or total to appear and a control will be displayed accompanied by a label.

- Calculations can be entered directly into the control which total a particular field across all records of the report eg. entering =Sum([Times Borrowed]) will calculate the total number of times that publications have been borrowed.

Other calculations using a constant such as =[field name]*0.75 can also be entered.

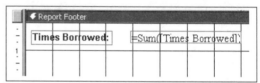

Note: All field names used in calculations are surrounded with square brackets ([ ]).

For more complex calculations the Expression builder is used. To do this select the control and click on the **Properties** button on the **Toolbar**, choose the **All** tab and click in the **Control Source** box and on the button which appears alongside. The Expression Builder will appear and calculations can be entered as described in Section 4.4.

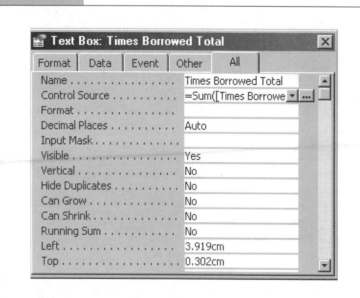

- The label can be renamed so as to reflect the contents of the calculated control.

- To check that the calculation works as required choose **Print Preview** from the **View** menu. Clicking on the button in the bottom left corner of the report window will display the last page of the report and the result of any calculations. Choose design view to further refine your Report.

Adding Group Headers and Footers

Group headers and footers are usually used to highlight groups of records. Often a description of the group is included in the group header and total values for the group included in the group footer.

To add a Group Header or Footer:

- Choose **Sorting and Grouping** from the **View** menu and the following dialogue box will be presented:

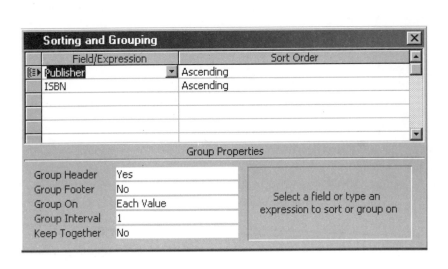

- Select the field you wish to highlight in the group header or footer and choose the required sort order.

- The Group Properties displayed in the lower part of the dialogue box determine whether a group header or footer is displayed. To display a group footer click on the choice **No** alongside the **Group Footer** property, click on the down-arrow which appears and choose **Yes** from the pop-up menu. Group Headers can be displayed in a similar manner.

Note: The name of the section will be titled with the name of the field and the word header or footer.

- To have Access calculate totals for particular fields across all records of the group use the method described above in **Adding Summary Totals and Calculations to a Report**. The only variation is that controls should be created in the group header or footer section. For example, Group Footers can be used to calculate the total number of times particular types of publication have been borrowed.

Group headers and footers can be deleted by reversing the creation process described above. However, if you delete a group header or footer any controls which have been added to these sections will also be deleted.

7.0 Saving

The database as a whole includes tables, queries, forms and reports. Unlike most other programs, particularly databases, Access saves these database objects into a single file which was titled when the database was created.

When entering data, saving of each record occurs when moving on to a new record.

Saving the entire database, including any tables, queries, forms and reports, occurs automatically when the database is closed or another database opened. However, each of the database objects can be saved to the database file independently at any stage. You will be prompted to save anyway when any object is modified and subsequently closed.

To save a particular object use the **Save** or **Save As** commands from the File menu, titling the object as necessary.

Objects in the database window can be renamed by selecting the object, choosing Rename from the Edit menu and entering the new name in place of the old.

8.0 Printing

You may have noticed an option under the File menu called Print. DON'T use this just yet. First you must decide what you want to print and how you want the print out to appear.

Decide what you want to print by displaying it in a window on screen. You may print a table, a query, a form or a report, in either normal or design view. Check how your print out will appear by previewing it.

Choose **Print Preview** from the **File** menu. This provides you with a bird's eye view of the page and is very useful for checking page breaks and the positioning of fields, controls etc. Use the navigation buttons in the bottom left hand corner of the window to move through the pages of your work. Point and click to take a closer look at a particular area; click again to zoom back out. When you have finished previewing choose the appropriate view from the **View** menu.

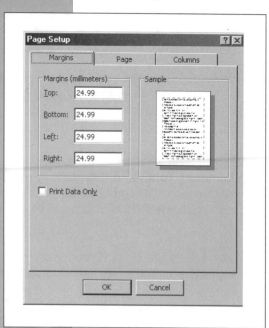

It may be that what you wish to print does not fit on to a page. Perhaps when printing a form each record is divided into several pages or the columns to the right of a datasheet are printed on to another page. There are several possible solutions to this problem:

- Decrease the width of any columns (assuming you are printing a datasheet).

- Rearrange and resize the controls so that they take up less space on the page (assuming you are printing a Form or Report).

- Use the **Page Setup** command from the **File** menu to:

Decrease the width of any margins using the **Margins** tab.

Switch from portrait to landscape (sideways) orientation using the **Page** tab.

Again you might like to check the Print Preview before finally printing.

Lastly, choose **Print** from the **File** menu. A dialogue box similar to that shown below is presented:

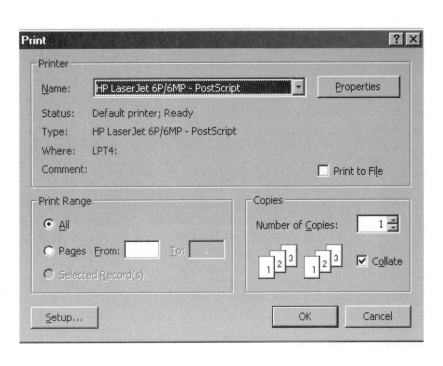

In the print dialogue box you can choose to print all the document, the currently displayed page, or a specific range of pages. To print a range of pages click on the **Pages** button and enter the first and last page numbers into the **From** and **To** boxes provided. To print all pages up to a particular page type the page number into the **To** box. To print all pages after a particular page type the page number into the **From** box. To print a single page type the page number into both boxes.

Click on the **OK** button and your data will be printed. How long it will take to print depends how many other people are also printing and the complexity and length of your print out. If you have waited more than 15 minutes. Seek assistance.

Hint: As a short-cut to printing, and if you have previously chosen the print set-up you wish to use, just click on the button on the Toolbar.

APPENDIX A

Importing and Exporting

Moving data to and from other programs is extremely useful since it allows you to mix the capabilities of Access with the specialist features of other programs such as spreadsheets, graphics or wordprocessing programs. It also avoids both the labour of re-typing and the possibility of introducing errors.

Importing Data

The basic procedure for importing any file into Access is the same:

• Create and title a new database file.

• Choose the Get External Data from the File menu and Import from the sub-menu. In the dialogue box presented choose the source of the data. If this is not another Access database then you will have to change the **Files of Type** box to the format you wish to import. Click on the **OK** button when this is complete.

Note: Consult the Office Assistant for information on file types that Access can import.

• Follow the Import Wizard instructions to complete importing of the database.

Exporting Data

• Open the Table, Query, Form or Report that you wish to export.

• Choose the **Export** command from the **File** menu.

• In the dialogue box presented choose the file format that you wish to export to from the **Save As Type** box choose the destination of the data and click on **Save**.